NEW
EVERY
MORNING

MEDITATIONS ON HIS DAILY GRACE

by CARA TRANTHAM

When Scripture is abundant in our lives, we will then be able to

USE IT WISELY TO ENCOURAGE &
BENEFIT FELLOW BELIEVERS,

HAVE A HEART FILLED
WITH PRAISE,

&

LIVE A LIFE THAT EXUDES
GRATITUDE.

The Word of God

We have access to the very words of God! Because the Bible is so common, it is like the air we breathe — a privilege that we can easily take for granted. We demonstrate our gratitude to God for His Word by letting it dwell in us "richly"! This word richly is also used in Titus 3:5-6. God tells us that He has poured out the Holy Spirit on us richly. And in 2 Peter 1:11, He says that He has richly provided an entrance into heaven for us. Perhaps two of the greatest benefits of salvation, outside of Jesus Christ, are the Holy Spirit and the promise of heaven. These gifts are so valuable that a price cannot be put on them! In the same manner, let us fill our lives with the richness of Scripture, allowing it to penetrate every area of our lives. When Scripture is abundant in our lives, we will then be able to use it wisely to encourage and benefit fellow believers, have a heart filled with praise, and live a life that exudes gratitude.

COLOSSIANS 3:16

—

Let the word of Christ dwell richly among you, in all wisdom teaching and admonishing one another through psalms, hymns, and spiritual songs, singing to God with gratitude in your hearts.

VERSES TO REFERENCE

—

TITUS 3:5-6
2 PETER 1:11

The Bride of Christ

We as the church have the privilege of being called Christ's Bride. Isaiah 61:10 says, "I will greatly rejoice in the Lord… for He has clothed me with the garments of salvation, He has covered me with the robe of righteousness, as a bridegroom decks himself like a priest with a beautiful headdress, and as a bride adorns herself with her jewels." Ephesians 5:22-23 compares the love of a husband and wife to the relationship between Christ and His church. We represent Him. We get to claim Him as our Husband. We get to share life with Him — our greatest joys and our deepest sorrows. We not only have the privilege to be acquainted with Him, but to know Him intimately. Let us thank Him every single day for this privilege, and commit to acting like the bride of our Savior.

Lord, thank You for choosing us as your Bride. Thank You for loving us even when we do not love You like we should. You are the most precious relationship we have! Help us to invest time in Your Word and make spending time with You a priority. Teach us how to pray and communicate with You. May we walk worthy of this privilege and calling.

COLOSSIANS 3:15
—

And let the peace of Christ, to which you were also called in one body, rule your hearts. And be thankful.

VERSES TO REFERENCE
—

ISAIAH 61:10
EPH. 5:22-23

EVEN IN THE FACE OF TRAGEDIES WE CAN WORSHIP AND PRAISE THE unchangeableness —— of God ——

The Kingdom of God

With earthquakes and tsunamis and world disasters constantly wreaking havoc around us, it would appear that there is nothing we can trust to remain. Life is unpredictable at best and volatile at worst. We can find comfort in the fact that the kingdom that Christ brought to earth, the one that we work for every day, cannot be shaken. Even in the face of tragedies and calamities, we can worship and praise the unchangeableness of God. He is our firm foundation when everything around us is sinking. We can have confidence that the work we are devoting our lives to will not see ruin, because our rewards lie above (Matthew 6:20). We simply have the opportunity to bring the kingdom of God to earth. As we allow God's authority to dictate our lives and determine our actions, we will show the world what a life surrendered to God looks like. In this way we reverence the King whose dominion can never be thwarted. Your kingdom come, Lord, Your will be done, on earth as it is in heaven (Matthew 6:10).

HEBREWS 12:28

—

Therefore, since we are receiving a kingdom that cannot be shaken, let us be thankful. By it, we may serve God acceptably, with reverence and awe,

VERSES TO REFERENCE

—

MATTHEW 6:10
MATTHEW 6:20

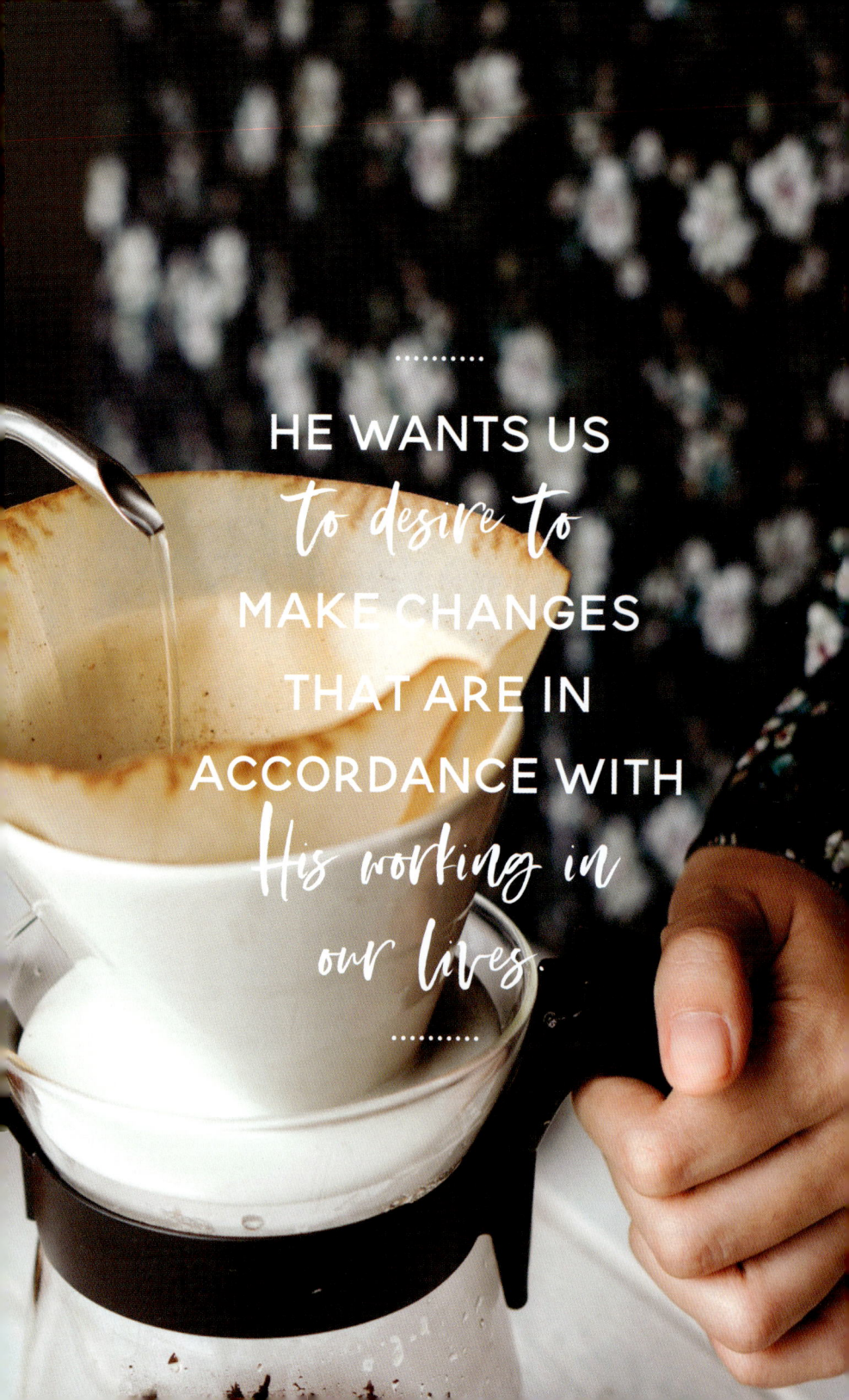

HE WANTS US *to desire to* MAKE CHANGES THAT ARE IN ACCORDANCE WITH *His working in our lives.*

The Steadfast Love of God

"Steadfast love" is also translated as "lovingkindness" and "mercy." All of these words are wrapped up together. "Kindness," "favor," and even the word "reproof" lies in these definitions. This can seem confusing, because often the world associates love with nothing but sweet words. But in order for God's love to be steadfast, it means that it endures the test of time. This is the never-ending and pursuing love of God for His people that endures. Even His words of correction, rebuke, and admonition are given in love because He wants our hearts to change. He wants us to desire to make changes that are in accordance with His working in our lives. He wants us to be listening for the Holy Spirit's prodding. He wants us to be so in tune with Him that we know His voice. When we get to the place where we interpret everything as gifts from His hand, we will know the depth of His steadfast love. And then we will be able to do nothing but praise Him.

I CHRON. 16:34

Give thanks to the Lord, for he is good; his faithful love endures forever.

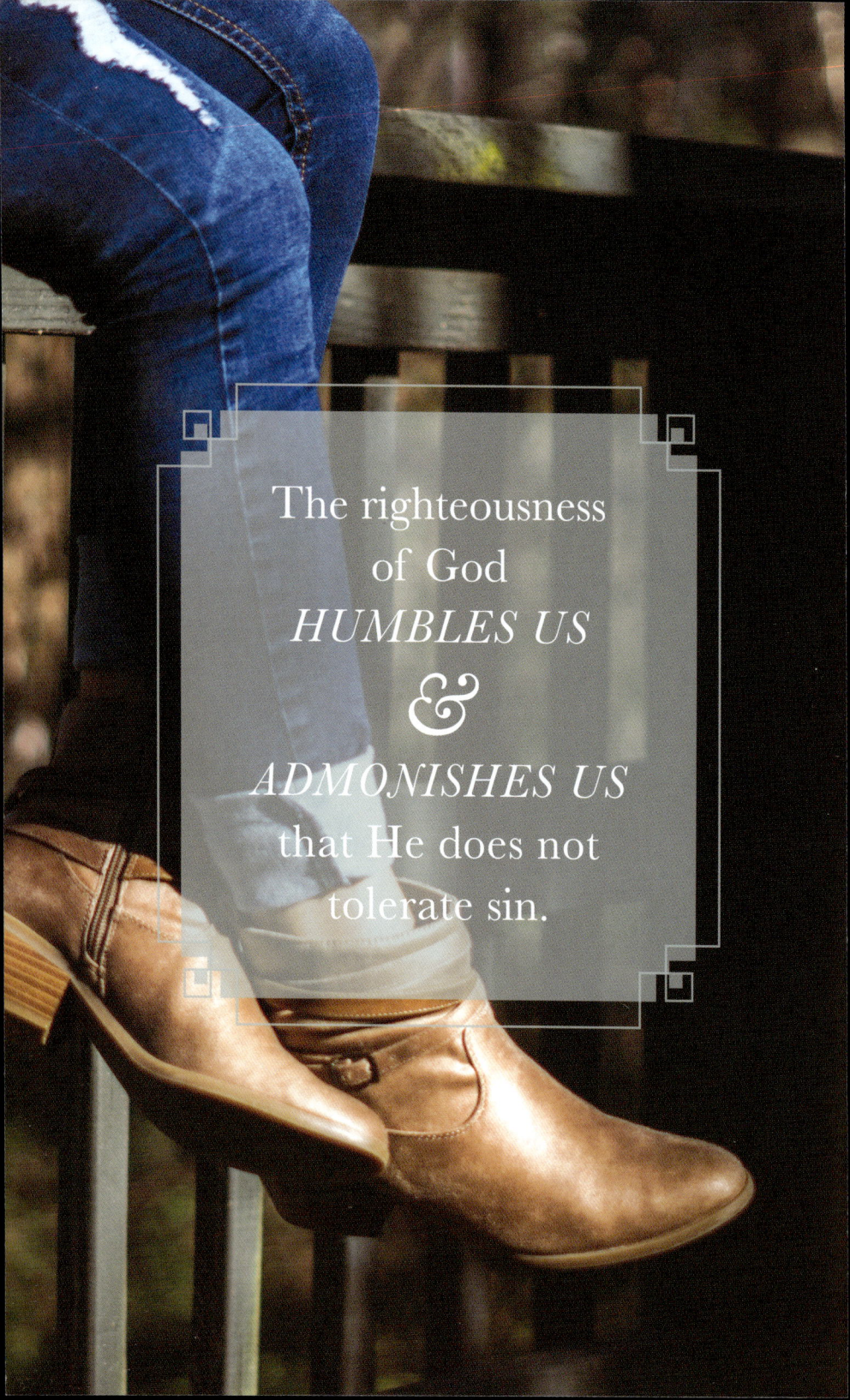

The righteousness
of God
HUMBLES US

&

ADMONISHES US
that He does not
tolerate sin.

The Righteousness of God

Aren't you so thankful that we can rest in the righteousness of God? God is righteous in His very nature, and He cannot deny His character. He will never do anything that is opposite of who He is. Psalm 145:17 says that He is righteous in all of His ways and holy in all of His works. The word "righteousness" here means "integrity, virtue, purity of life, rightness, correction of thinking, feeling, and acting." The righteousness of God humbles us and admonishes us that He does not tolerate sin. This is something we can praise Him for, because it leads to pruning in our lives and constant conviction in areas where we fall short of His holiness. We can find joy that He loves us too much to leave us in our sin! God's standard is high because He knows we cannot do this on our own. We have access to His grace and help to get us through. This is a high calling for believers, but we stand under the power of God who is all of these and makes these attributes available to us through Jesus. Thank Him that we don't have to rely on our own righteousness. Thank Him that we can depend on His.

PSALM 7:17

I will give to the Lord the thanks due to his righteousness, and I will sing praise to the name of the Lord, the Most High.

VERSE TO REFERENCE

—

PSALM 145:17

Recount His wonderful deeds in your life

The Wonderful Deeds of God

PSALM 9:1

—

I will thank the Lord with all my heart; I will declare all your wondrous works.

Have you taken time recently to look back and "recount" the things God has done? His goodness to you, His goodness to others, His goodness on your behalf? His deeds are wonderful. To say that He does wonderful deeds means that He does the extraordinary. He does hard and difficult things. He can accomplish the things that seem out of our grasp and reach. This also means that sometimes, the things He does will seem harsh and less than good. But it is all for the end result of reaching the goal of sanctification. You've heard it said that before something gets better, it has to get worse? Sometimes, this is where we find ourselves walking the tension of freedom and grace. God allows us to sit in the awful so that we will experience the wonderful. Sometimes, He allows us to wallow in the mire of sin so that when we experience His grace, it will hold us captive in ways that it wouldn't have otherwise. Recount His wonderful deeds in your life. Look back at all He has done — the good and the bad — and thank Him for the story of redemption He is weaving through your life.

We can
rejoice even
in the middle
of heartache
because we
know who
He is.

The Protection of God

The word "strength" here means "might in material, physical, political, social, or personal ways." The Lord is our strength in all these areas. We can lean on Him for wisdom in social situations, for political decisions, and in personal circumstances. He is also our shield of protection from sin, from the world's allures, from even our own understanding (Proverbs 3:5). Our heart, our will, our emotions, passions, and appetites can trust Him, that He knows what He is doing with our lives and our circumstances. We can be confident that He will surround us with protection, aid, and ultimately bring Himself glory through our lives. We can rejoice even in the middle of heartache because we know who He is. When we lift our voices in praise and thanksgiving, we confess that He is ultimately in control. The word "thanks" here in Hebrew is *yadah*, meaning "to cast." I imagine a fishing rod casting its bait far out into the water. Thanksgiving is a tool to destroy the lies that we so often believe. We can use the bait of gratitude to discover and identify our fears, insecurities, worries, and anxieties, and then in turn cast them at the feet of Jesus.

PSALM 28:7

—

The Lord is my strength and my shield; my heart trusts in him, and I am helped. Therefore my heart celebrates, and I give thanks to him with my song.

VERSE TO REFERENCE

—

PROVERBS 3:5

The holiness
of God
DESIRES to
DWELL, REST,
and LIVE
in us.

DAY 8
The Holiness of God

Another way to define "holy" is "sanctuary," which is a reference to where God dwelt with His people in the Old Testament. The tabernacle was the tent-like structure that traveled through the wilderness, and the temple was the permanent structure built once the children of Israel reached the Promised Land. Once Christ came, He fulfilled the law and ushered in a new period of grace. His death on the cross meant that people no longer had to make sacrifices for their sin. The amazing thing about this is that the body of Christ is the temple in which Christ now dwells (1 Corinthians 6:19). The Holy Spirit permanently dwells in the church after salvation. The holiness of God desires to dwell, rest, and live in us. This is only possible because of the blood of Christ. His sacrifice made us right before God, and now we live out of gratitude for what He has done for us.

Because He couldn't be in the presence of sin, He made atonement through His Son so that we could fellowship with Him. I am thankful that He is higher and more holy than we are. His holiness is our sanctuary.

PSALM 30:4
—
Sing to the Lord, you his faithful ones, and praise his holy name.

VERSE TO REFERENCE
—
I COR. 6:19

WITH EVERY FORGIVENESS, GOD
GIVES A FRESH START AND A CHANCE
TO BEGIN AGAIN

The Glory of God

This psalm is a tribute of praise to the Lord for delivering David from some difficult situations. It may refer specifically to the time when David disobeyed the Lord's command and numbered the people anyway. David's punishment resulted in an epidemic that killed 70,000 people. This psalm expresses David's sorrow and repentance for his arrogance, for thinking he knew better than God did. Once David humbled himself before the Lord and was forgiven, David felt free to praise, despite all the death and grief around him. With every forgiveness, God gives a fresh start and a chance to begin again. Like David, we have been forgiven of much! This does not mean that we will never have consequences for our choices. He doesn't promise to replace sorrow with joy, but He will transform our grief into joy (John 16:20). It means that even in His discipline, God is kind and gracious. His chastening means that He loves us and wants our attitudes and behaviors to be only for His glory and for our good. He is after His glory, and He will not compete with anyone else for it. Everything He does is toward this end, and His glory should be our priority as well. May we never be silent in giving Him glory!

PSALM 30:12

—

so that I can sing to You and not be silent. Lord my God, I will praise You forever.

VERSE TO REFERENCE

—

JOHN 16:20

Shout for joy, you heavens! Earth, rejoice!

ISAIAH 49:13A

Songs of Praise

Music comforts. Music causes celebration. Music is powerful, and God created it to be that way! Isaiah 49:13 says this: "Shout for joy, you heavens! Earth, rejoice! Mountains break into joyful shouts! For the Lord has comforted his people, and will have compassion on his afflicted ones." Even nature was created to praise Him. Music is a means by which God desires for us to exalt Him. Singing is not just something we do at church during a worship service. Music should be integral in our lives, giving Him praise all week, no matter what day it is! There is a lot of music out there that does not honor the Lord, and it can be easy to overlook it and just let it play subconsciously in the background. But when we intentionally use and make music to honor and glorify the Lord, it does something for our hearts as well. Not all of us can sing and play an instrument, but thank God for those who can! May we use this expression of praise whenever we have the opportunity and give Him gratitude for this creative avenue to worship Him.

PSALM 33:2

—

Praise the Lord with the lyre; make music to him with a ten-stringed harp.

VERSE TO REFERENCE

—

ISAIAH 49:13

May we never *use His Name lightly* or *take for granted* the honor we have to call on *His glorious name.*

The Name of God

"I love the name of Him Whose heart Knows all my griefs and bears apart; Who bids all anxious fears depart, I love the Name of Jesus. That Name I fondly love to hear, It never fails my heart to cheer, Its music dries the falling tear; exalt the Name of Jesus." — W.C. MARTIN

PSALM 44:8

—

We boast in God all day long; we will praise your name forever.

The personal name for God in the Old Testament was a four letter word, *YHWH*. Because it was so holy, the translators of the Pentateuch didn't want to write this word out in its entirety, so they used this abbreviation or replaced it with the name *Adonai*. There are many different names for God, each describing one of His attributes or character traits. He is *El Shaddai*, the Lord God Almighty. He is *El Olam*, the Everlasting God. He is *Jehovah Tsidkenu*, the Lord Our Righteousness. He is *Jehovah-Rapha*, the Lord That Heals. He is *Jehovah Shammah*, the Lord Is There. He is *Jehovah Jireh*, the Lord Will Provide. He is *Jehovah Shalom*, the Lord Is Peace. These names are precious because they express who Christ is. May we never use His Name lightly or take for granted the honor we have to call on His glorious name.

HE IS

—

EL SHADDAI: *The Lord God Almighty*
EL OLAM: *The Everlasting God*
JEHOVAH TSIDKENU: *the Lord Our Righteousness*
JEHOVAH-RAPHA: *The Lord that Heals*
JEHOVAH SHAMMAH: *The Lord is There*
JEHOVAH JIREH: *The Lord Will Provide*
JEHOVAH SHALOM: *The Lord is Peace*

He is *always* good. In the *best* of times. In the *worst* of times.

The Goodness of God

God is good. We hear and use this phrase quite a bit! What do we mean by it? We make this blanket statement, usually in reference to positive news, miracles, and things that go our way. We don't hear this in conjunction to tragedies, misfortune, and heartbreak. But if we believe the Word, His steadfast love endures forever. He is always good. In the best of times. In the worst of times. We can trust that His deliberations and the things He allows are all truly good at their core. They may not seem good, but we can trust that in His steadfast love, He will work it together for good for those who love Him (Romans 8:28). The word "good" defined as an adjective means "to be desired or approved of." The amazing thing about our God is that He doesn't need our approval. He doesn't need us to evaluate whether His actions are good or not. One of the words also translated as "goodness" is "better." As it relates to God, isn't this so true? He is so much better to us than we could ever deserve! We can worship Him despite how our circumstances look and trust that He can do nothing but good.

PSALM 54:6

—

I will sacrifice a freewill offering to you. I will praise your name, Lord, because it is good.

VERSE TO REFERENCE

—

ROMANS 8:28

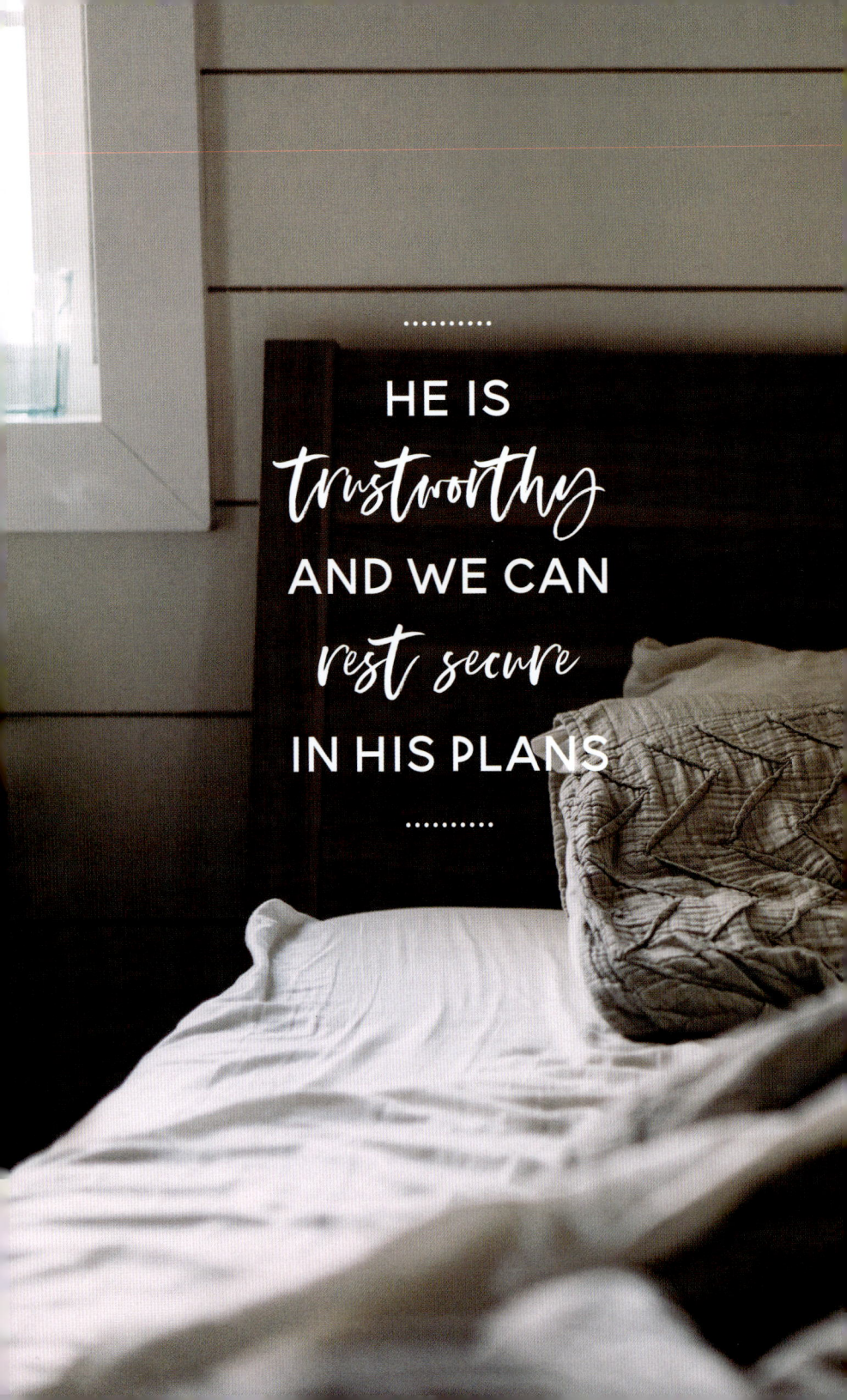

HE IS

trustworthy

AND WE CAN

rest secure

IN HIS PLANS

God's Sovereignty

What a great comfort it is to know that God is absolutely free to do what is best! And, it may seem odd, but not only am I grateful that He works for my good, but I am even more thankful that He works for the good of all of His people! I love that this is not a me-centered universe. When we can stop to realize that even though things in our lives may not be going the way we want, we can have confidence knowing that He is indeed working behind the scenes, not just for our happiness, but to accomplish His purposes in the world. He is looking out for my ultimate best, and your ultimate best, and that person across the sea's ultimate best. He is trustworthy, and we can rest secure in His plans and know that He will always do what is best for His people.

Lord God, we are so thankful for Your sovereignty that assures us that we don't have to make the world spin on our own. Thank You for being in control and not us. Help us to trust your sovereign hand.

PSALM 57:9
—

I will praise you, Lord, among the peoples; I will sing praises to you among the nations.

He continues to stretch out His hand to us

IN BLESSINGS,
PROVISIONS,
& MOST OF ALL,
IN SALVATION.

The Nearness of God

The word "incline" used in Psalm 116:4 describes the Lord drawing near. Hidden in this singular word are multiple adjectives that describe the Lord's posture to us. He continues to stretch out His hand to us, in blessings, provisions, and most of all, in salvation. He has given us the Holy Spirit to guide us, and as we walk with Him, we are walking hand in hand with the Lord. The King of the universe stoops to bow down to His creation, not in worship, but in relationship. He bends to listen to us. He holds out and extends His hand to us so that we may grab it and walk with Him through this life. Isaiah 55:6 says to seek the Lord while He may be found and call upon Him while He is near. "Near" indicates an intimate acquaintance. Someone we talk with often. Someone we have deep affection for. Let us never allow His nearness to become stale! May we rest in the amazing truth that God is near and seek Him through His Word and prayer each day. He is not far from us. He is near.

PSALM 75:1

—

We give thanks to you, God; we give thanks to you, for your name is near. People tell about your wondrous works.

VERSES TO REFERENCE

—

PSALM 116:4
ISAIAH 55:6

The Lord Our Shepherd

PSALM 79:13
—

Then we, your people, the sheep of your pasture, will thank you forever; we will declare your praise to generation after generation.

Sheep are known for being rather dumb animals. They are really stubborn. They think they know the best way. They are always getting stuck, getting lost, getting into problems because they think their way is best. They are not content where the shepherd has put them, so they try to go to better pasture somewhere else.

And this is the way the Lord describes us. We are sure that our own way is best, always looking for something better somewhere else, believing the lie that God is holding out on us. But He is our Shepherd. He cares deeply for each of us. He builds fences, not to control us, but because He wants to keep us safe. He moves us to different pastures, not to cause us sadness, but because He knows better grass is there. He is good in all of His ways to us. And for this, we give thanks. When He leads us to unfamiliar territory, we give thanks. When He says no to our requests, we give thanks. Because we can rely on the Shepherd to give us the things we need and to say no to the things that will harm us. And because He is our Shepherd, we will never want for anything.

He stands GUARD over our affections.

The Keeper of Our Hearts

God is the Creator of our hearts, the sustainer of our being, and the One who knows us better than anyone else. He knows the things that will satisfy us. He knows the things that will harm us and lead us away from Him. He is protective of our hearts. The Bible even says that He is jealous for us. He is righteously jealous when we turn to things instead of Him to fill us. And so He stands guard over our affections. The practice of being thankful will also steer our hearts in the right direction. It will remind us where all good things come from and anchor our hearts to the One who loves us more than anyone else.

Jesus, thank You that You are jealous for our hearts. Thank You for loving us enough to not give us everything we want. Thank You for breaking off relationships that have severed us from You. Thank You for closing doors to things we have asked for, because You knew those jobs and opportunities would squeeze You out. Thank You that we can trust You to guard our hearts.

PSALM 86:12

—

I will praise you with all my heart, Lord my God, and will honor your name forever.

PSALM 121:5

—

The Lord protects you; the Lord is a shelter right by your side.

He has allowed us to be partakers of His divine plan.

The Opportunity to Witness

PSALM 105:1

—

Give thanks to the Lord, call on his name; proclaim his deeds among the peoples.

It is an amazing thing that despite all the ways God could spread His gospel, He chose to use us! He doesn't need us to accomplish His purposes, but He has allowed us to be partakers of His divine plan. He uses sinful humans, jars of clay (2 Corinthians 4:7), to show off His glory. We can praise Him for the way that He has allowed us to worship Him as we share the good news with the world. How beautiful are the feet of them who preach the gospel of peace (Romans 10:15)! God thinks it is beautiful when we put aside our own agendas and desires in order to fulfill the Great Commission. What an honor this is! It is a privilege that we get to be an extension of His grace — His hands and feet to the human race.

When was the last time we shared His deeds with others? When was the last time we stopped talking about the weather and began talking about Jesus? When we realize the magnitude of the responsibility and privilege we have, we will find great joy in the opportunity to witness.

VERSES TO REFERENCE

—

ROMANS 10:15
2 COR. 4:7

We can count on Him to continue loving us steadfastly.

The Faithfulness of God

The faithfulness of God is something we can count on at all times. We never have to worry that He will change His commitment to us. We can count on Him to continue loving us steadfastly—without variation. Lamentations says that His mercies are new every morning (3:22-23)! We can be sure that the sun will come up every day. And if the sun comes up everyday, we can be sure that His faithfulness to us will not cease. We give thanks to His Name because He will never fail to forgive us, to give us grace, to love us, to care for us. His provision will never fail.

Because He will never fail, we can trust He will keep His promises. This does not mean that He will give us everything we want. He is not faithful to build the Kingdom that we want, but to exalt His Name and His Word above all things. He will not be mocked (Gal 6:7), and He will not allow anything or anyone else to be supreme. That includes our desires. He will fulfill His promise of faithfulness to us for His Name's sake.

PSALM 138:2

—

I will bow down toward your holy temple and give thanks to your name for your constant love and truth. You have exalted your name and your promise above everything else.

VERSES TO REFERENCE

—

LAM. 3:22-23
GALATIANS 6:7

MAY WE NOT SPEND TIME IN HIS WORD SIMPLY AS HABIT, OR AS SOMETHING WE SHOULD DO, BUT AS SOMETHING THAT WE CANNOT *NOT* DO.

The Chance to Draw Near

Because of God, we have the chance to draw near! Jesus' sacrifice on the cross gave us passage into the Holy of Holies. The veil was torn when God's Son paid the price for our sin so that we could enter into His presence. When God looks at us, He sees Jesus' blood and not our sin! He has separated us from our sin as far as the east is from the west. When He created us, He desired to know us and fellowship with us. Let us remember this privilege and spend time with Him as often as we can. May we not spend time in His Word simply as habit, or as something we should do, but as something that we cannot *not* do. May it be the highlight of our day to sit in quietness with Him, drinking in His nearness. We are so unworthy, but because of Jesus, He has made us worthy in His eyes. We may draw near and bring Him our thank offerings, and give Him our very bodies as an expression of our gratitude (Romans 12:1).

2 CHRON. 29:31

—

Hezekiah concluded, "Now you are consecrated to the Lord. Come near and bring sacrifices and thank offerings to the Lord's temple." So the congregation brought sacrifices and thank offerings, and all those with willing hearts brought burnt offerings.

VERSE TO REFERENCE

—

ROMANS 12:1

God's Perfect Timing

God is never too late. He is never behind. He is never waiting too long to answer your request. He is always right on time. We can trust that He knows best. We can trust that if He is withholding an answer from us, it is for our good. He may be doing something in your life in the wait, or He may be doing something in another area, but you can be sure that He is not sitting by silently. There is a purpose in your waiting.

Time is limited to us, but God is outside of time. In His eternity, He has already done it. We just cannot see it yet, and we cannot see how it will all play out. But we can wait for Him, because His Name is good. We can trust that our timetable is not the only factor in His decisions. He works things according to His will, and this is comforting to us when we feel forsaken and forgotten. We can say with confidence that He is only good, in all of our waiting.

PSALM 52:9
—

I will praise you forever for what you have done. In the presence of your faithful people, I will put my hope in your name, for it is good.

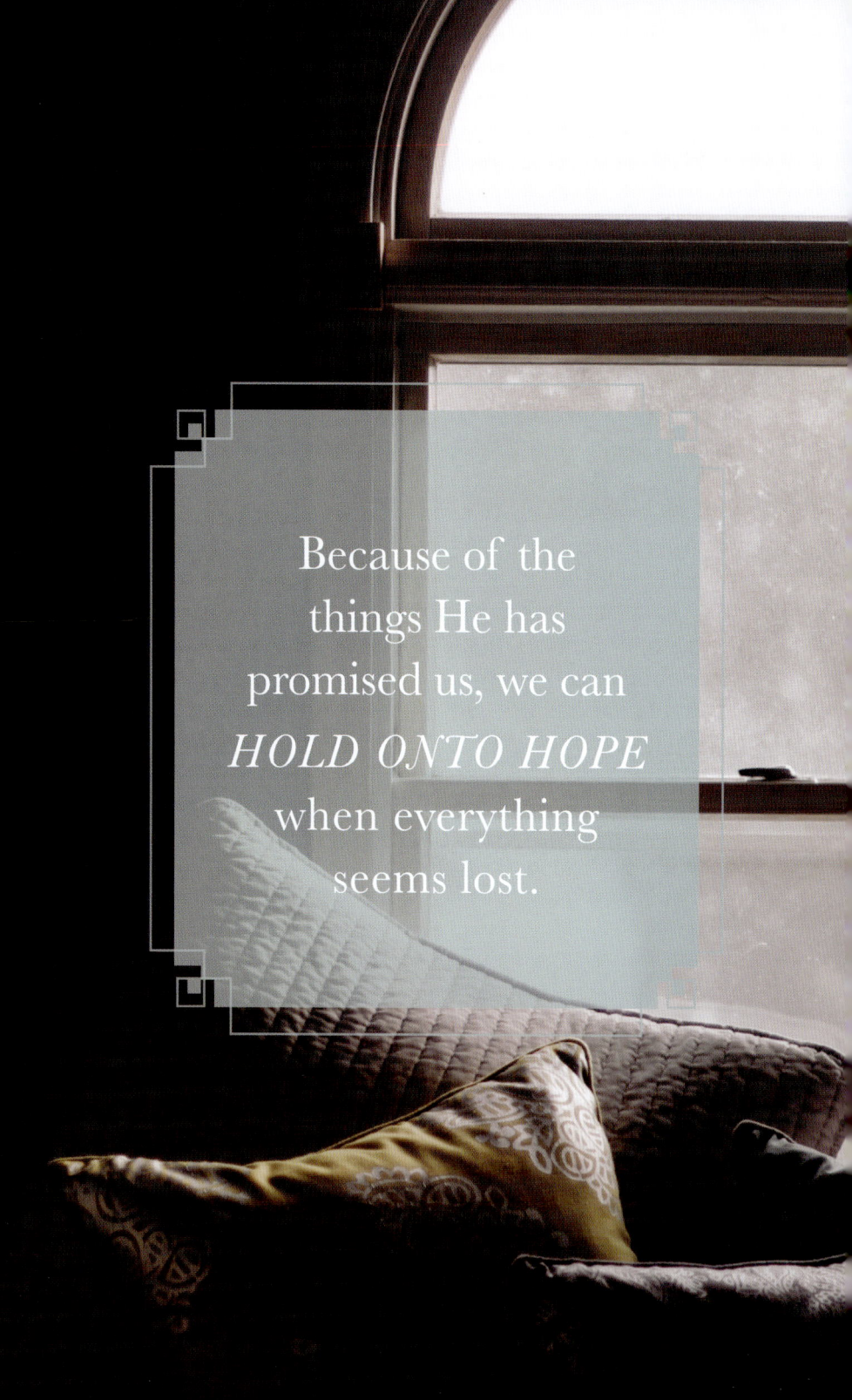

Because of the
things He has
promised us, we can
HOLD ONTO HOPE
when everything
seems lost.

The Promises of God

Do you have a favorite promise from the Bible? Have you claimed any of them or prayed the promises of God? His promises are vast and far-reaching. There is great joy to be found in them. Because of His promises, we have cause to celebrate and rejoice. It is in these promises that we find life, and hope, and cause to persevere. Without the promises, we would easily be defeated, discouraged, and disheartened. Because of the things He has promised us, we can hold onto hope when everything seems lost. We can grasp onto His goodness even when our circumstances don't dictate it. He says, "I will never leave you or forsake you" (Hebrews 13:5). He will give eternal life to anyone who asks (John 3:16). He promises to hear us when we call (Isaiah 65:23). "All things work together for good to them who love Him" is a promise that no matter how bad things are, He is working behind the scenes to redeem it (Romans 8:28). Every promise finds completion in Jesus, and we can rest in Him. How thankful we should be for these sweet reassurances of His love and care!

2 COR. 1:20

—

For every one of God's promises is "Yes" in him. Therefore, through him we also say "Amen" to the glory of God.

VERSES TO REFERENCE

—

ISAIAH 65:23
JOHN 3:16
ROMANS 8:28
HEBREWS 13:5

HE WANTS
TO HEAR OUR
Requests, OUR
Worship,
OUR *Joys*.

The God Who Hears

The God that we serve is a God who hears us when we call. Not only does He hear us when we pray, but He encourages prayer! And not exclusively when we need something, and not conditionally when we are praising Him, but all the time. God does not have selective hearing. He is all-in, for the good and the bad. He wants to have a relationship with us. An everyday, common, familiar, intimate relationship. Any relationship requires communication, and our relationship with God is no different. He wants to communicate with us through His Word, and He wants us to talk to Him through prayer. He wants to hear our requests, our worship, our joys. The way we can show gratitude to our God who hears is by being people who listen for Him in return. It requires spending time with Him and being in His Word. It requires seeking Him in all things and acknowledging Him in all our ways (Proverbs 3:4-6). Will we be people who hear?

JOHN 11:41

—

So they removed the stone. Then Jesus raised his eyes and said, "Father, I thank you that you heard me."

VERSE TO REFERENCE

—

PROVERBS 3:4-6

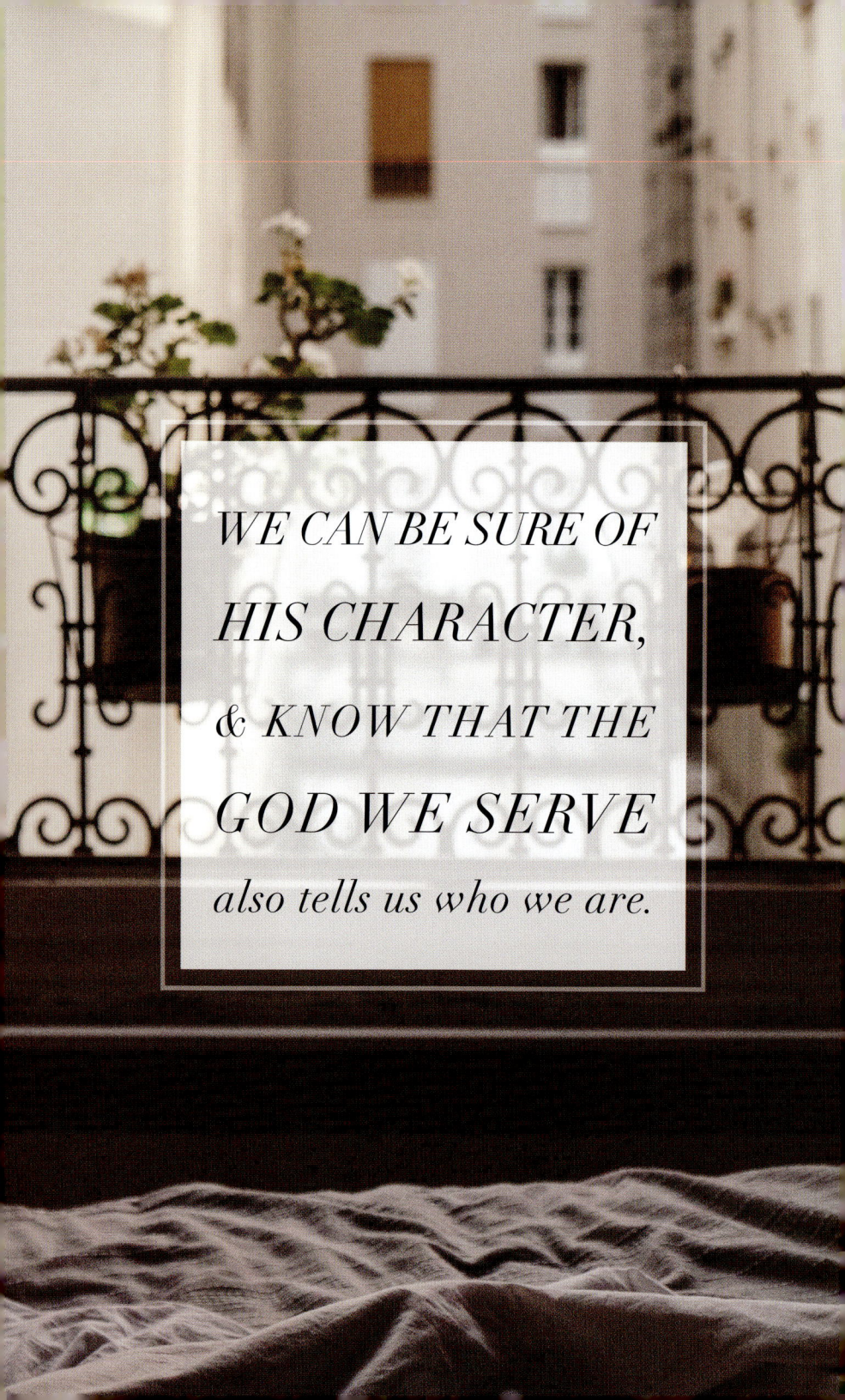

WE CAN BE SURE OF

HIS CHARACTER,

& KNOW THAT THE

GOD WE SERVE

also tells us who we are.

The Character of God

If we say that we believe the Bible, we must believe everything in it. Paul says it this way: "We thank God constantly for this, that when you received the Word of God, which you heard from us, you accepted it not as the Word of men but as what it really is, the Word of God (1 Thessalonians 2:13).

Of all the things the Word of God is to us, the most important thing it does for us is tell us who God is. This is precious because when we know who God is, we can be confident in His guidance. We can be sure of His character and know that the God we serve also tells us who we are. If we didn't know Who God was, how would we ever know that we could trust Him? But as we read His Word and see the promises He made to His people and how faithful He was to His people, we can say with confidence, "You have dealt well with your servant, O Lord, according to Your Word" (Psalm 119:65).

REVELATION 1:8

—

"I am the Alpha and the Omega," says the Lord God, "the one who is, who was, and who is to come, the Almighty."

VERSES TO REFERENCE

—

PSALM 119:65
1 THESS. 2:13

We are not pawns on a chess board, but rather willing and grateful servants.

The Appointment of God

I am grateful that He has a purpose for each of us, that our lives mean more than just surviving and having a good time. I am thankful for the opportunity to serve Him in His Kingdom. What a privilege! We are not pawns on a chess board, but rather willing and grateful servants. He knows our strengths and talents, and He knows what we will develop later in life and how we will use these things specifically. Because He knows our uniqueness, He appoints us ministries based on our specific talents and gifts. And once He has given us these appointments, He also gives us the strength to fulfill our mission. We are not on our own to figure out the rest. He gives us creativity and freedom in how to use these giftings, but He will help us along the way and give us opportunities to use these talents for His Kingdom. Let us be thankful that He has considered us faithful to work in His fields.

Lord, show us where You have appointed us to Your service. Show us through Your Word the places where we can fill the gaps in the body of Christ. Make us faithful to Your service.

I TIMOTHY 1:12

—

I give thanks to Christ Jesus our Lord who has strengthened me, because he considered me faithful, appointing me to the ministry

We can run this race in the strength of the Lord

The Great Cloud of Witnesses

Who is the great cloud of witnesses? It may be the heroes listed in Hebrews 11. It could be the saints who have gone before us. Many of us have ancestors who passed on their faith to us. We get the picture that these witnesses are in the box seats cheering us on. The ones who went before have run this race, and they know what we are up against. They know we can run this race in the strength of the Lord.

The beauty of the church is that it is, as a whole, a team. We come around each other, comforting those in pain, helping up the fallen brother, encouraging those who think they can't go any longer, running alongside the weaker ones, giving water to the worn out. This passage specifically mentions prayer as being one of the greatest support systems there is. We can sponsor our team and equip each other to be victorious by praying! Yes, we will experience the final victory because Christ has already won that, but how thankful we are that He has provided us the daily victory if we lean into His strength.

2 TIMOTHY 1:3

—

I thank God, whom I serve with a clear conscience as my ancestors did, when I constantly remember you in my prayers night and day.

We can lay hold
of this promise that
HE WILL NEVER

CHANGE.

The Unchangeableness of God

Just imagine — a person who was always the same! Never sad, never tired, never grouchy. But our God is that person. He doesn't change His mind or His mood or His motive. We can be confident that He will always be there and always be the same. He will not stop forgiving our sins, and He will always love us. He will not change His opinions. He is just, and because that is who He is, He cannot be unjust. He is not a referee — He doesn't miss anything, and He doesn't make bad calls. He sees it all, and He treats us all the same. He doesn't have favorites. He will never decide that we are no longer worthy of grace. We can lay hold of this promise that He will never change. He will not and cannot change His nature.

Lord, thank You for always being the same. Thank You that we never have to figure out what You're doing, because we know that You are doing what You always do — loving, sustaining, forgiving, restoring.

JAMES 1:17

—

Every good and perfect gift is from above, coming down from the Father of lights, who does not change like shifting shadows.

There is
little that is
sweeter than
the peace that
Jesus gives.

The Peace of God

There is little that is sweeter in the Christian life than the peace that Jesus gives. How is it possible that martyrs, burning at the stake for their faith, show no sign of fear or anxiousness? This is the peace that passes understanding (Philippians 4:7). It is a rare and beautiful thing that the Lord gives peace to His children, no matter what evil is swirling around them. We can be alone against the world, and yet we can feel no anger or bitterness, because we know that the world treated Jesus the same way. We can withstand words that wound us and still maintain our peace. We can face death and illness, knowing that we have the presence of God.

Lord, allow us to take advantage of this peace You offer us. Remind us to come to You when our souls are overwhelmed. Thank You for the gift of Your peace.

PHILIPPIANS 4:6-7

—

Don't worry about anything, but in everything, through prayer and petition with thanksgiving, present your requests to God. 7 And the peace of God, which surpasses all understanding, will guard your hearts and minds in Christ Jesus.

VERSE TO REFERENCE

—

PHILIPPIANS 4:7

As we give our attention
to a life of *continual
communication with God,*
we will find more *reasons
to be* THANKFUL.

The Gift of Prayer

When the veil in the temple was torn, we were given immediate access to the Holy of Holies. No longer do we need to go through another man to talk to our Heavenly Father. We no longer need to rely on someone else to tell us what God says, because we have His Word and we can take our questions and petitions straight to Him! The word "watchful" here means "active," and in another place we find the admonition to "pray without ceasing" (1 Thessalonians 5:17). As we give our attention to a life of continual communication with God, we will find more reasons to be thankful. We will see His hand more clearly in our everyday lives and have cause to thank Him. We also can find great comfort in the gift of the Holy Spirit, who intercedes in prayer for us when we are at a loss for what to pray. Not only does our God make Himself accessible in prayer, but He offers Himself to live inside of us to aid us in praying.

Lord, thank You so much for this unspeakable gift of prayer. May we avail ourselves often of it, to confess our sins, present our petitions, and most of all, to adore you and praise Your Holy Name.

COLOSSIANS 4:2

—

Devote yourselves to prayer; stay alert in it with thanksgiving.

VERSE TO REFERENCE

—

I THESS. 5:17

THERE ARE OPPORTUNITIES
ALL AROUND US TO SERVE
LIKE JESUS DID.

The Opportunity to Serve

No matter what stage of life we find ourselves in, we always have the opportunity to serve someone. We may be housebound, but we can make phone calls and send cards. We may be part of the workforce, but we cannot only do our work well but do it with grace. We may work hard without ever seeing a paycheck, but the Lord sees our hearts and rewards us as we faithfully and willingly serve. There are opportunities all around us to serve like Jesus did. Another area we can serve others is in what we say, whether giving encouragement or loving criticism. And not only do we serve in His Name, but we give thanks while we are doing it! Cleaning toilets, taking someone to the bathroom, gathering trash—He asks us to give thanks even for the dirty jobs.

Lord, help us to see everything we do as a gift to You! May we realize that You have given us responsibilities in order to learn more about You, and to use our gifts well. May we sweep up Cheerios gratefully, clock in eagerly, and be on the lookout for how we can serve those around us. Remind us that there are no menial jobs in Your sight.

COLOSSIANS 3:17

—

And whatever you do, in word or deed, do everything in the name of the Lord Jesus, giving thanks to God the Father through him.

Knowing Christ is worth so much more than anything else we could have.

The Generosity of God

As if salvation wasn't enough, the Lord so graciously pours out blessings generously on us everyday. None of us deserve life, good health, financial stability, or happiness, and yet, so often we enjoy all of these things! God didn't owe us salvation, and He most certainly doesn't owe us the material things that we enjoy.

It can be hard to remember this when things start going poorly. It's easy to become entitled and angry when He takes things away from us that we are used to having. What if, instead, we counted the loss of these things as a gain for Christ's Kingdom? Philippians 3:8 says, "Indeed, I count everything as loss because of the surpassing worth of knowing Christ Jesus my Lord. For His sake I have suffered the loss of all things and count them as rubbish, in order that I may gain Christ."

If you're in a season of plenty, give thanks to God for His incredible generosity! If you find yourself in a season of drought or loss, thank God for incredible generosity! And thank Him for His presence that cannot be taken away. Paul says that knowing Christ is worth so much more than anything else we could have in this life.

2 COR. 9:11-12
—
You will be enriched in every way for all generosity, which produces thanksgiving to God through us. For the ministry of this service is not only supplying the needs of the saints but is also overflowing in many expressions of thanks to God.

VERSE TO REFERENCE
—
PHILIPPIANS 3:8

When we
count our blessings,
we soon stop counting
our problems.

The Amazing Grace of God

The word "grace" is also translated "favor, pleasure, and thanksgiving." Isn't that fascinating? "Grace" and "thanks" are synonymous, because the graces that He pours out on us will produce thanksgiving in us. With each grace that He bestows on us, we should, in return, give gratitude. His goodwill and lovingkindness to us are graces, yes, but so is any delight, charm, or sweetness we may find in this life. All is grace from the Father's hand.

When we count our blessings, we soon stop counting our problems. When we begin to see everything around us as a grace, even the things we would prefer to ignore, we find that even the bad is grace, because of the end result of leaning more on Jesus. In this, too, we can find mercy to deliver us from evil, faithfulness to walk with us through our trials, and the restoring of our souls. We find through hard times that He keeps His promises (Joshua 21:45), He gives us strength in our weaknesses (2 Corinthians 12:10), and He gives joy to the full (John 15:11). These are also graces.

Lord, may Your grace extend to more and more people. May we be vessels that You use to show the world Your amazing grace. Thank You for this amazing grace that saved wretches like us!

2 COR. 4:15

—

Indeed, everything is for your benefit so that, as grace extends through more and more people, it may cause thanksgiving to increase to the glory of God.

VERSES TO REFERENCE

—

JOSHUA 21:45
JOHN 15:11
2 COR. 12:10

FOR STUDYING GOD'S WORD WITH US!

CONNECT WITH US:

@THEDAILYGRACECO

@KRISTINSCHMUCKER

CONTACT US:

INFO@THEDAILYGRACECO.COM

SHARE:

#THEDAILYGRACECO

#LAMPANDLIGHT

WEBSITE:

WWW.THEDAILYGRACECO.COM
